CODING FOR KIDS SCRATCH

The Ultimate Guide for Beginners to Learn Coding Skills, Create Fascinating Games and Animations

Thomas Poe

The information herein is offered for informational purposes solely and is universal as so. The presentation of the information is without a contract or any type of guarantee assurance.

The trademarks used are without any consent, and the publication of the trademark is without permission or backing by the trademark owner. All trademarks and brands within this book are for clarifying purposes only and are owned by the keepers themselves, not affiliated with this document.

TABLE OF CONTENTS

Introduction

Scratch is a visual programming language that creates a safer learning experience for various age levels. It helps to build immersive media-rich ventures, including animated tales, book reviews, science projects, simulations, and games. Visual programming of Scratch helps you to discover fields of knowledge that are otherwise unreachable. It offers a comprehensive collection of multimedia methods to create groundbreaking applications that you can use. You can do it quicker than other programming languages. In various ways, Scratch promotes problem-solving strategies that are important in all aspects of life, not just coding. The world needs immediate feedback, helping you to easily and reliably evaluate your logic. The visual system makes it easy to observe the movements of processes and improve your way of thinking. The concepts of software engineering are rendered available from Scratch. It strongly motivates research, facilitates the quest for understanding, and enables realistic learning through exploration and discovery. If just the imagination and novelty restrict the threshold, the barriers to entry are very minimal.

These principles are successfully taught in a realistic and motivating way to students. In standard algebra lessons, students typically feel no emotional connection to the concept as they study about variables. Whereas when they study the variables in Scratch, they will easily use variables in very practical ways, to regulate the pace of the animation or keep track of the score in the game they are creating.

Students will also learn about the design process when working on Scratch projects. A student typically begins with a concept, makes a prototype, experiments with it, debugs it when things go bad, get guidance from several other people, and strengthens it and redesigns it. It's a periodic vortex: have an idea, create a plan that can contribute to more plans, new projects, and so on.

Chapter 1: coding-an overview?

There's a lot of publicity around coding, so let's start by explaining what coding is. I mentioned above that when I first witnessed the source code on a web page, I thought I was looking at the language that my computer was communicating with. It is a typical way to describe what the code is, but that isn't valid. The computer may not grasp the complexities of the language. In reality, only words that the computer recognizes quite well are "Yes" or No." Imagine that you are constructing a bridge with a squad of engineers. You're on one side, they're on the other, and you have to interact to finish the tasks. The thing is, your mobile has crashed. You can communicate with them by using a torch. One flash for the yes, and two flashes for no. It will require some time, but the bridge will finally be completed. That's how a computer interacts with humans. The computer's language is the binary code, the mathematical one and the zero. Much like a torch, there are just two choices. The machine knows "on and off," and there's nothing more. So, until you type one and zero strings into the text editor, you're not writing code in your computer's language. But if the code isn't written in the programming language, what will you be doing?

Computer Code is a Language

Imagine writing the code just like that. You cannot speak binary, and the computer can't get any closer to knowing the human languages. If you want to instruct the computer on what to perform, you need to build a translator to serve as an intermediary. That's the intention of the code. Code is a type of writing that is not binary, that is simple to learn and comprehend for humans, and that computer can also interpret. For several of the applications you're likely to be operating with, the code you're creating is simply a step away from its binary code that the computer will process. You're going to write a code that comes from human language. The programs that are installed into your computer transform what you have written into binary. It's because you wanted to communicate to someone who just spoke in Mandarin, you know English, and the only interpreter you might locate talked only in French and Mandarin. You'd need another interpreter to convert from English to French, and then the first interpreter would translate French to Mandarin, ideally without context being wasted in the process. What kind of blows my brain has to do here seems to be that somehow it functions. We have software that converts programs for a computer that only communicates binary. It is an incredibly complicated operation, but writing human words on the computer that speaks binary here I am. For instance, there is a lot more to this, but these are the important things you need to learn before you begin a code conversation with the computer.

1.1 Creative computers

Computers are fast:

Computers are extremely powerful. You'll do wonder when you understand how to use the power of computer programming correctly. The addition of two figures, which may be as large as a billion each, hardly takes a nano-second for today's modern computer. Read this again, Nano-Second! This implies that a computer will run about a billion advertisements in 1 second. Would it ever have been done by any humans? Ignore a billion ads per second; average people can't even get ten additions per second. Computers thus are giving great speed.

Computers are cheap:

If you're a stock market dealer where you had to keep track of thousands of data, you can trade them effortlessly. If you had to do it manually, imagine the difficulty it could bring. It's almost unlikely. The price will be adjusted when you measure this stock output. The other choice is to hire workers so that new supplies can be monitored in parallel. This means that the cost is going up sharply. If some of the staff make a miscalculation within the process, do not understand the difficulty you will have to face. You could end up wasting your money! Contrast that with the case when a computer is being used. Computer systems can manage a huge volume of information easily and effectively. In the new world, a hundred stocks are nothing in front of a computer.

Computers can run 24x7:

Without getting exhausted, computers can operate 24x7. So, if you have a task that's large enough, you can allocate it to a computer by programming it and sleeping peacefully without fear.

1.2 Programming languages

There are hundreds of coding languages out there. Several languages are all-purpose or multipurpose, but most of them serve a particular role. CSS, for instance, mostly functions, making things appear pretty. JavaScript, a comparatively older language, operates to render websites more responsive. There are advanced languages that are perfect if you need anything technical, but there are a few basic languages that you need to get started.

HTML

To open any web page, it costs you two code lines written in HTML. Brief for Hypertext Markup Script, HTML is used as the skeleton of the Internet. It instructs the web pages what must be shown and when and how they match the style sheet. It also instructs your browser where to search for content, including photos and videos you'd like to use in your project, and where to locate the style sheet you're working on.

One point to be aware of:

Theoretically, HTML is not a "programming language," so it does not use logic-based expressions as, let's assume, Python does. HTML is a markup language—but just like the coder vs. programmer vs. developer debate—you're certainly not mistaken to call this a programming language, particularly when you're new.

CSS

The CSS is your style sheet. If you open a CSS file, you'll see several references to colors, font formatting types (like bold, italics or underlined) and family fonts. (like bold, underlined, or italics). As your browser loads a tab, the HTML states, "Let this section of the page appear like a header. Okay? "It also states, "Here's where to look to learn what the header might look like." It is still going to be a CSS format.

JavaScript

JavaScript is a language that adds interactivity to a web page. For instance, when you press the button on the website, it's JavaScript, making the button appear as you click it. Controls for the animations and web-based video players are mostly JavaScript.

Ruby" versus "Python

Both of these programming languages are mostly used to build web apps.

In other words, they build programs that enable web pages to do stuff at a high level of interactivity. E.g., if you want to construct a bot to establish an automated payment system for the customers, you'll use one of them. They're fantastic to work and learn with because they're highly flexible.

1.3 Why children need to learn programming with this book

Because it requires a visual approach, coding is much easier and clearer to comprehend. The great thing about this is the ease that it brings to learning by eliminating all the complex programming components. Children no longer have to think over a forgotten semicolon or a missing bracket. It helps them develop their critical and logical thinking skills.

We also think that coding will unlock the path to a better future for our children and that if they would not study how to code now, it will be much less complicated to find a job one day.

Thus, initiatives such as Scratch, which have been developed excitingly and colorfully, are a perfect way for our children to start learning critical skills like computational reasoning, creativity, algorithmic logic and problem-solving.

Scratch is indeed an exciting and creative activity.

Scratch for children helps children to think outside the box. Also, the projects they create are interesting and entertaining, making studying process a thrill.

Builds reasoning and logical thinking abilities

One of the great aspects of Scratch coding for children is that it improves their critical thinking. By addressing different problems, they encounter, children naturally master the techniques of problem-solving.

Scratch is visually attractive

Having your kid involved in programming isn't a problem with Scratch, as it's extremely pleasing to watch. It helps children to picture the coding, making the whole thing more fun and exciting.

Easy to comprehend

One of the main problems of coding would be that it takes several resources to be completely mastered and learned. However, that's not the case now. The language was developed for children, it's simple to understand. Children don't require complex texts, manuals, and tutorials to understand how the language operates.

Fully Accessible

Almost everyone can make use of Scratch, and the only thing they need is internet connection. So by switching towards Scratch for kids, you can provide your child with a good education in coding from the comfort of your home.

Good extensions of hardware

If your kid wants to spend time and energy on useful stuff, then Scratch is ideal. Several companies are designing hardware sets that combine with Scratch to build fun designs. Kids, For example, Makey-Makey and Microbit, encourage kids to design and develop their game controllers.

Serves as a programming intro

When starting with Scratch, children get a glimpse of what the programming seems like. From there, they will grow their expertise and spread out into different niches according to their preferences. Later, they get a bachelor's degree in computer engineering and probably learn multiple languages. Scratch for children is also a perfect launchpad for teenage brains.

1.4 Coding is used nearly everywhere

From entering your name to playing a song, anything you do on your computer requires coding. But how can machines comprehend what they were told? The exponential technical progress we've experienced over the past few years has had a far-reaching influence on how it operates. You don't need to dig beyond the horizon to see where the many important developments have taken place. Computers have substituted millions of normal work hours and warehouses with analog computers with quicker, safer and more efficient solutions.

Since computers are operating on code, it's obvious why you can access it everywhere. Computers will begin to substitute old and outdated systems of anything from microwave ovens to power plants. And the role of code in our everyday lives is going to grow.

1.5 Coding as a career option

Software developers could quickly see themselves serving major businesses like Apple, as well as they could in a hospital or even an automotive company.

How is computer programming essential in the future?

Programming is important for studying how to evolve, developing very environmentally sustainable alternatives to global challenges, and so on. Essentially, it helps to speed up the phase of outputs and inputs in a computer. Besides, it lets you improve the ability to collect, automate, handle, interpret data and knowledge correctly.

Programming is, without any doubt, really significant. Hundreds of colleges, thousands of teachers, students and professionals studying, learning and performing programming disciplines are the strongest testimonies to this. And this is why programming seems to be the talent you've got to master.

Many of the important factors why programming is essential are as follows:

- The interaction with computers and machines

- Integrating the power of coding in all human ventures

- Automation of operations

- Development of machine intelligence

We may only further wonder whether programming is relevant now and would be important in the future. What we should do, though, is focus on why programming is critical to programmers.

If you're dreaming of being a programmer, you ought to consider that there's a lot to remember. If you're curious how much you're going to get paid when you're a programmer, you're in the correct place. We took data from PayScale, Glassdoor and Salary.com to include average figures. Take into consideration that this amount is an approximation, not an assurance.

We've picked out the most common programming fields and used the details for web developers, web designers, game developers, and smartphone developers.

If you get to be a web developer, the main responsibility you would be given is to create and manage web apps. It's a complex area – the particular task always depends on the language the users know. It can classify you into a back end or front-end developer – or a full-stack when you understand both of them. Glassdoor sets annual salary at $94,000 a year, significantly more than the PayScale ($59,000). However, Salary.com says an average of 61,000 dollars. But it just relies on the kind of site you're employed at.

Chapter 2: Scratch; a digital new friend

2.1 The term 'scratch.'

The word Scratch derives from the phrase "Scratching" in music. Using older recordings on a turntable, DJs scrape fresh rhythmic sounds to make new remixes and tracks. As almost all the Scratch projects are publicly accessible for usage and modification, sections of programs created by some other Scratchers will effectively build new projects. In the Scratch internet world, there are programmers of all ages who can name, comment, post, remix, and download any programs they build and upload to the website.

2.2 How Scratch works

Scratch is a programming language created to introduce programming to kids by encouraging them to build creative animations and games. About 15 million projects reside in the public database of the Scratch system. Scratch is the language focused on blocks: users control programming blocks. Since the eighties, block-based languages did exist but have recently seen acceptance as methods for teaching programming. Many other studies have demonstrated that languages focused on blocks are effective as programming teaching tools. Previous studies, including Scratch applications' static study, evaluated implementing different programming principles to Scratch initiatives. In a recent study, we noticed that lengthy scripts and code replication limit a beginner programmer's capacity to comprehend and alter Scratch programs. By snapping the blocks together, Scratch enables young programmers to build programs. Scratch comprises a programming language composed of various blocks and an easy-to-learn graphical creation framework that provides a visual design tool and built-in sound editing functions.

Along with sound files and graphics, Scratch also comes with large sets of sample programs, many of which you can use to build your Scratch creations. They are constructed of blocks of graphics that are placed together. And the manner that they clip together, the scratch blocks imitate puzzle bits. Scratch blocks should be snapped together only in forms that make sense, stopping them from being used in invalid configurations by fresh programmers. In this way, Scratch imposes the correct syntax of programming and guarantees that beginners understand the correct way to assemble programming logic and formulate it. The creation of Scratch was influenced by the process used by hip-hop DJs to mash up and mix records to make unique and different tracks. In Scratch, programmers can build the latest application projects that combine pre-built blocks' code, sound files and graphics in all sorts of unique combinations. Scratch enables programs to be changed on the fly by programmers, enabling improvements to be made even though the Scratch application operates. The outcome is an engaging programming experience that promotes creativity and learning.

2.3 Creating a Scratch account

All you need to do is hit the Scratch site, then sign up for the service using your email address to run it. On the upper right-hand line, click Enter Scratch. You will be presented with an attend up screen

Generate your username and password and click the Next button to get to another screen

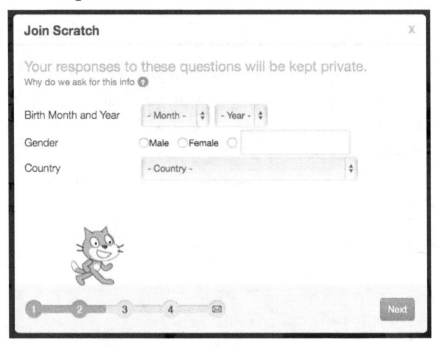

Type in the personal details that Scratch uses to track users using this site. Click on the Next button to step forward

Join Scratch   X

Enter your email address and we will send you an email to
confirm your account.

Email address

Confirm email address

1   2   3   4   ✉   Next

Please include an email address, and you will receive
confirmation through email. If you want to share the designs, you
need to pick a link in your email address (if you don't want to
share it, you can go without doing it, but every time you log in,
you'll get a notification at the top of the page).

You will see the welcome screen after accessing the email account
and choosing Next.

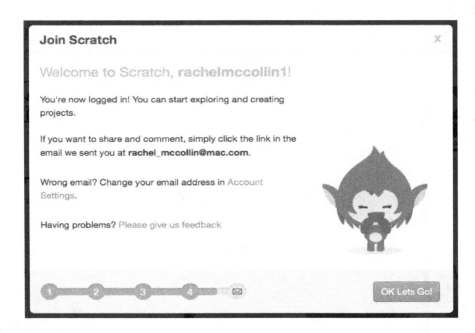

Join Scratch ✕

Welcome to Scratch, rachelmccollin1!

You're now logged in! You can start exploring and creating projects.

If you want to share and comment, simply click the link in the email we sent you at **rachel_mccollin@mac.com**.

Wrong email? Change your email address in Account Settings.

Having problems? Please give us feedback

1 — 2 — 3 — 4 — ✉   OK Lets Go!

If you click "Ok let's go!" you'll notice the home screen including details of what's going on in the Scratch Community, including activities by people you meet or log in to your account.

2.4 Features

You can use the application offline and online. You may download the browser if you wish to run it on your device without internet connection.

2.5 Applications and sites

Scratch is provided for free on the Scratch website (http:/scratch.mit.edu), and Scratch Application is also readily available for download on any smartphone or computer. It works and looks the same on macOS, Windows, and Linux. Besides,

Scratch projects on the Scratch app can also be made offline. It was particularly created for young adults aged 8 to 16 years of age (from second grade to junior highschool); however, people of all ages can interact with Scratch. It has the equipment to build games, engaging tales, simulations, graphics, artwork, and more by utilizing block-based programming.

2.6 The Scratch user interface

The screen has been separated into several panels: the stage and sprite list on the right, the blocks palette on the left, and the scripts section in the center. The block palette has pieces of code-named blocks, and you can move them from that palette to the scripts region to create programs. The palette is organized into block groups to keep the palette ordered and simple to use. There are blocks like motion, sound, operators, control, events, looks, variables, sensing and other blocks.

2.7 Significance

Scratch is still generally and widely used to teach fundamental computer programming to children in schools worldwide. Some teachers use Instructor Accounts to track pupils in the Scratch Group. With Scratch, children and adults acquire an awareness of programming principles and then switch to many different programming languages as their interest is established. When using Scratch, people can not only build and remix ventures, but they can also work with many Scratchers on different projects.

Scratch allows kids to build imaginative thinking, analytical reasoning, and interactive learning, which are essential qualities for surviving in the modern era. In today's civilization, the ability to develop computer programs is an important part of education. When practicing to code in Scratch, children often study critical strategies and methods for problem-solving, task planning, and communication ideas. From primary school to university, and through computer sciences, mathematics, social sciences, and arts, children study Scratch across all ages. Certainly, the primary goal is not to educate people as professional work programmers but to nurture a modern generation of creative minds who use programming to effectively express their ideas.

Chapter 3 Getting started with the Scratch

In developing the language, the developers' key goal was to make the language and programming experience easy, clear, and comprehensible for children who had not tried programming before.

3.1 The Scratch installation

Go to http:/scratch.mit.edu. Tap the home section, and then press

3.2 The components of the Scratch

Your scratch screen or scratch software components are the following:

- Main Tabs

- Block palette

- The Stage

- The Sprite list

- Main Tabs

- The Tools

Script area

You will need to move between the Scratch Editor's three major tabs when you build the project/games. These sections enable you to code, modify the sprites' appearance, or allocate a sprite with a sound. The coding tab enables the dragging of code blocks into the coding region. Click the Costumes tab to customize how the sprite appears. Via the Sounds tab, you can integrate the latest sound into the project.

Stage

The screen is your stage. It's just like the sprite, but it is unable to move. It does have settings, named backdrops, rather than costumes. The stage is where you will see your tales, games, and animations brought to life. The stage is called the project's

background; like a sprite, it may have backdrops of numerous costumes, sounds, and scripts. Four hundred eighty pixels wide and 360 pixels tall is the level.

Each sprite has a certain location on the stage, but since the stage is always on the backplate, not a single sprite may switch behind it.

Sizes of Stage

There are three common stage sizes:

Regular

Standard mode; 480 to 360 pixels for the level.

Small Stage Layout

The stage size is half the standard size, with a resolution of 240 to 180 pixels, which is beneficial in getting more room in scripts.

Full-screen mode

It matches your player to the user's web browser's current resolution.

Sprites

All the projects are made of 'sprites,' two-dimensional objects and photographs connected with their codes. Scratch has a huge sprite library. You can either pick one to utilize in the project or draw a picture manually in the built-in paint editor. You can even use an image file already stored on your device, or you can also draw a photo on paper to import the picture to the computer and then incorporate it into the Scratch project. It is easy to make a sprite look like anything you desire. It might look like a pet, a banana, any text, or even your best buddy's photo, or you might be able to draw a lovely fictional character.

Sprites, either generated by the developer, uploaded or displayed in the sprite's library, are the key objects that execute all of the actions in a given project. While the stage may also be built in a project, since only sprites are movable, most projects include at least one sprite.

Scratch helps its users bring the sprites to life in numerous forms, just as flipping them in the air, using text balloons to make them think or speak words or phrases, and letting them produce sounds, shrink, expand and alter costumes.

Script

Sprites may have several and stack command blocks named scripts. By joining individual command blocks altogether in a stack, scripts are constructed. Scratch can run your blocks from top to the bottom when you click on the script. The computer begins from the top and runs one after another the commands that you tell it. A script can be very brief or very lengthy (only three to four blocks long). Maybe a sprite has just one script, several scripts, or even no script at all. A single sprite can have several scripts that are started by a similar event. In that case, all the scripts would be performed collectively.

Acting with scripts is convenient. The following guidelines could help you:

To build a script and arrange it meaningfully, you just have to drag the Block Palette blocks into the script/code region.

Blocks are moved further to assemble them; except for the Hat Blocks, they may be inserted below or in some other block.

To dis-assemble them, the blocks must be moved away from each other.

Right-click the hat block to remove the script, click delete, or drag and drop the script in any block palette.

To start a script, click on it.

You may modify the Stage Scripts and each Sprite in the Scripts tab.

Block Palette

The components are utilized to code the sprite to perform or state something. You need to give a series of guidelines to your computer to execute while programming, such as 'play a tone,' 'go down,' and go up.' Such instruction in Scratch is called the command block.

The simple building blocks you're going to play with are

command blocks. To build guidelines, you pin them along on the screen, just like Lego® bricks. Each block instructs the computer to do actions when the command is implemented. There are many kinds of blocks, identical to Lego®. Many blocks add the numbers together, some perform sounds, monitor the operation and execution of other blocks, and some allow things to move on the monitor.

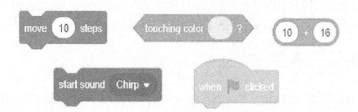

All blocks are color-coded to keep it a bit clearer to figure out what each block does. Orange blocks, for example, are the control blocks; they inform the computer where the instructions should start or stop. Blue blocks are motion blocks; they specify how and when to move the sprite.

Block Categories

Scratch version 3.0 has 119 blocks in it (without extensions):

Motion blocks

These are the blocks which control the movement of a Sprite. In Scratch version 3.0, 17 Motion Blocks exist.

The following 15 Motion Stack blocks are presenting Scratch version   3.0:

- — It lets the sprite move the no. of steps in the forward direction where the sprite's face is.

- **turn ↻ ( ) degrees** — It lets the sprite turn in a clockwise direction for the defined amount.

- **turn ↺ ( ) degrees** — It lets the sprite turn in a counter-clockwise direction for the defined amount.

- **point in direction ( )** — It positions the sprite in the specified angle direction.

- **point towards ▼** — It positions the sprite towards another sprite or the mouse-pointer.

- **go to x: ( ) y: ( )** — It lets the sprite move to the given X (horizontal) and Y (vertical) position.

- **go to ▼** — It lets the sprite move to another sprite, a random position, or the mouse-pointer.

- **glide ( ) secs to x: ( ) y: ( )** — It lets the sprite glide to the provided X and Y location, taking as long as the specified time period.

- `glide ( ) secs to ( ▾ )` — It lets the sprite glide to another sprite, a random position, or the mouse-pointer, taking as long as the amount of time specified.

- `change x by ( )` — It changes the X (horizontal) position of a sprite by the given amount.

- `set x to ( )` — It sets the X position of a sprite to the provided amount.

- `change y by ( )` — It changes the Y (horizontal) position of a sprite by the given amount.

- `set y to ( )` — It sets the Y position of a sprite to the provided amount.

- `if on edge, bounce` — It flips the direction of a sprite over when the corner of the screen is touched.

- `set rotation style ( ▾ )` — It will set the sprite's rotation style.

The following 3 Motion Reporter blocks are available in Scratch version 3.0:

- **x position** — The sprite's X (horizontal) position.

- **y position** — The sprite's Y (vertical) position.

- **direction** — The sprite's direction.

3.3 Scratch variables

Variables are used to hold details for use in programs. The variable is a box of sorts that can hold one part of knowledge at a time, such as a word or a number, as a short review from earlier. Holding this piece of data helps us reference and change it in software at different places. This talent makes the variables highly useful!

Scratch will only save numeric values in a variable that can be moved to any program block space with a circular shape. Create a variable on the variables page and assign the tick box, based on how much you want the consumer to see and modify the value.

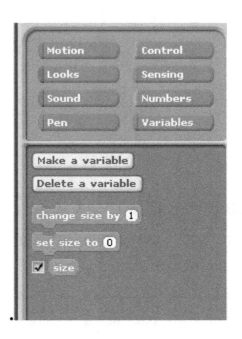

Most of the programming blocks have a circular slot where a number is inserted to decide how the command would perform. If required, each of these slots may be substituted with a variable. The following practice (from project variables) utilizes the size variable to evaluate the move command's size. The variable's value is modified within the loop so that the distance covered changes every time the loop is implemented. It enables the sprite to produce a design.

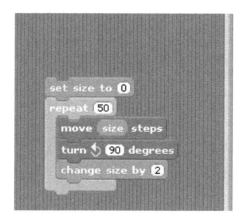

Notice that the variables may be modified by the program's final user if the checkbox stays checked on the variables tab. You should set the variable on stage and right-click it to determine the range of allowed values selected by the operator with slider control.

Make sure the programmers can describe and utilize variables within the sprite program. They should be allowed to build an applet that sketches a shape using a size variable that can be modified by the user while running the software.

The sprite rate in continuous motion may be regulated by a variable specified strictly for the sprite but not at the application level. The major sprite's speed parameter in the variable application is controlled with the ascending and descending arrow keys or by pressing the space to pause the sprite. Tapping the left and the right keys will change the position of the turtle, and this form of action is typical of video game asteroids (also called a Dyna turtle in Logo)

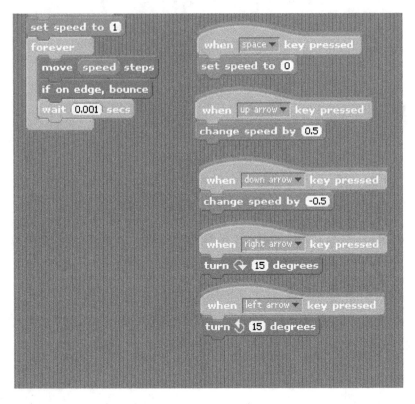

What differentiates a global variable from a local variable?

When you got to the crossroads, did you choose all the characters and only your sprite?

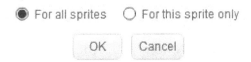

For all of the sprites, or only for this sprite: the true problem.

Variables have become universal as you choose for all sprites, meaning that they can be changed or reached by all sprites in the venture, regardless of the sprite created. On the other hand, if you select this sprite, the variable appears local. The local variable may be modified or often retrieved from the sprite where it was created.

For one thing, the web is global, and it's simple to reach anything saved online using any gadget in the world! However, if you save anything on your device's hard disc, consumers would not be allowed to access it on a new device because it has been saved locally.

Let's go forward and put them into practice now that we know the two major types of variables that we might have!

3.4 Loops in Scratch

Looping (or iteration) is a very critical term for programming.

Typically, most of the children's scripts have been very lengthy at this point of our Scratch ventures. Pieces are also repeated. The concept that we can ask the computer to repeat a series of instructions as many times as we want is very effective, but I think that children enjoy it because it involves less effort!

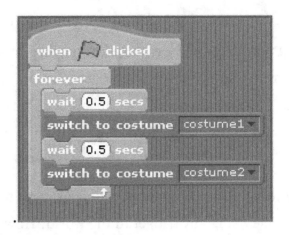

At this point, we could expand our bee-gathering pollen experiment by thinking about what the bee will do the next day and then looking at ways we could get the bee to replicate its route using a loop. Nevertheless, I think it's worthwhile to adjust the topic or design of these instructional pieces of learning Scratch. It makes the children engage in it. In reality, the use of loops encourages children to start integrating their ideas into their Scratch creations. It's a very strong source of motivation.

As a consequence, I normally add loops by displaying basic sprite animation. Some of the creatures, including Scratch, Parrot, Bat, Dog and many others, have costumes appropriate for animation. After importing the appropriate costumes (ask the kids if this is different from having a new sprite), I start by displaying the switch to costume block, asking the students how they can make it look like the wings are flapping..

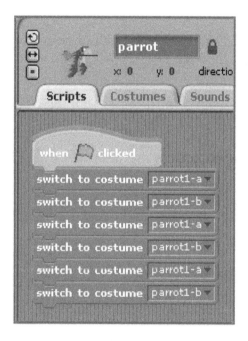

We're always going to wind up with anything like this. It makes a lot of sense. It indicates the concept of sequencing. If it doesn't work, that's all right. We're going to try again. We're going to persevere. Then why doesn't that work? If no one can answer (somebody normally does), I ask how long they think this script will require running through. How long will it take the computer to switch the costume? Try that if they can't explain anything. It doesn't take much time for anyone to say that the computer has to wait a while before switching the costumes.

It's better-the wings are flapping. A little slowly, maybe, but I'm sure the kids can find out yet how to speed things up a little.

It's all right to make mistakes. It's all right to test things out and then go back and make it work or work well. Kids love to do this.

So now it's the moment to introduce the strength of looping. Does anyone note something in this script?

Be sure you've been waiting long enough. Then ask her or him to split the script into the pieces which have been repeated Interactive whiteboards are great for this. Then I design how to wrap the forever loop all around the piece. I ask them what they suppose they're going to do. And sure enough, kids are doing as they thought.

Then I'm going to show them a repetitive block. I ask kids what this is going to do and what happens if I alter the number.

It is their move. It is a wonderful lesson that encourages children to take ownership of their interest from the beginning. There are a few sprites with sufficient outfits to animate-from a flapping bat to a biting shark. Some of them would like to create their own. Or maybe you'll apply a costume to a bee.

Count-Controlled Loops

Count controlled loops keep repeating code blocks several times.

Example 1

This program gives an output of the word **Hello!** Three times.

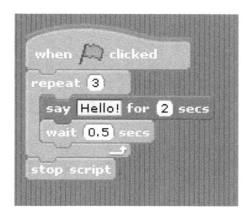

Challenge: Duplicate this program and modify it so that the client can choose how many times a message has been repeated. They should even enter a message that needs to get repeated. It is required to create two variables for achieving this. Variables would have to be fixed before the loop begins and should be put in the Say and Repeat blocks.

Example 2

The program counted from one to twelve and executed the numbers to stage.

Challenge no. one: Copy and adjust the program to count backward.

Challenge no. two:

Copy and modify the software so that the user could choose when to start counting. Fix the values of the counter variable relative to whatever they are entering.

Challenge no. three:

Introduce another variable into the program in the way that the client inserts two numbers before beginning the loop. The program should be counted from exactly the first number to the second. You're going to need the third variable to figure out how often to run the loop. By subtracting the first no. from the second no., you get the required value.

Challenge no. 4:

Compose another program narrating table times. The customer should be permitted to select which tables can be accessed. Make use of the connect blocks to create the details like you would while narrating time tables.

Challenge no. 5:

Write the latest program that only creates even numbers. The number will be even if it is divisible exactly by two numbers. You're required to use the IF block to perform.

Challenge no. 6:

Create another program that demands the consumer for a number and then narrates all the factors. The factors of a number are such quantities specifically divided into the number. The mentioned pseudo-code illustrates how you would be able to do this.

Chapter 4: Creating a plan for your project

4.1 Scratch games projects

Through scratch programming, there are several games coded. Here we can explore how to create the game by using it.

4.2 Why can Scratch be used to create games?

Scratch is among the best sites to create coding projects online, as previously described. It's a fantastic starting point to learn coding basics.

Scratch programming language seems extremely flexible. From creating simulations to sharing immersive tales, scratch blocks could be used for all. However, the most common usage of Scratch is to program video gaming.

If you join the Scratch forum (https:/scratch.mit.edu), you can continuously experience a variety of video games being improved and added. The Scratch programming language seems suitable for games since it encourages player input and allows players virtually infinite authority over its code.

4.3 What a game is perceived to be

We first have to understand what precisely a game is before we can create a game.

Among the most popular ways of entertainment today is gaming. There is a range of different video games played for fun, education, or both. Games follow two main criteria that must be fulfilled for anything to be called a game:

1. There needs to be something the player could have command of.

2. There must be a goal for the player to achieve.

It is indeed a game if anything follows both of these conditions!

4.4 Phases in the development of a game

Step no.1: Begin with the plan

The first and very crucial stage in creating a game is planning. You may even consider this as the design of your game.

This phase may seem to be insignificant, but it provides direction to the project. People who miss this stage and start coding without a strategy will quickly lose sight of their target and, before it is complete, sometimes eventually end up abandoning their game.

But don't worry! It can be exciting to create a strategy!

Planning is an ideal way to exercise your imagination and develop a unique idea for a project. While at first, it sounds intimidating, it can make the process quick by using three basic guidelines.

Step no 2: Choose a theme:

Discover what the gamer is trying to do

Step no 3: Select a goal to be achieved by the gamer

The rest of the game will proceed on its own after you sort out all of these three things. However, you don't need to work things out in this particular sequence! Perhaps the best thing is to select a theme and focus on the remaining two steps. You should do your best to keep things easy when you're designing your game!

Don't think about the first game if it wasn't what you expected it to be. Choose something you're going to achieve in either one or two hours since this will be more satisfying. Remember that it requires a lot of experience and hard work to build complex games such as those on Scratch Webpage.

Step no. 3a: Try to sort out the Visual Theme.

The visual presentation is one of the most significant factors of a game. It impacts the player's perception a lot. The visual style of the game is a mix of its characters and settings.

A historical themed game, for instance, will be held in an ancient fortress, with warriors and horses. A wild western game, with cowboys and a wine bar, will be based in the desert!

Picking a theme will also be the simplest part of creating a game since it follows when you decide on a concept that you want. To choose a style, try to sort out one element you would like to bring into the game.

There are some examples of ideas:

- I would like to create a game which is underwater.

- I would like to make a game with aliens and astronauts.

You can quickly extend all of these suggestions to become a full visual theme for both settings and character types.

Step no. 3b: Find out the main mechanism.

The next step in creating the strategic plan is to find out what

players will be doing in your game. To do something like this, you have to:

---

1. Firstly, find out how the players are going to control the game.

2. Then, you should work out what the target of your game would be.

When you're concerned about what players will do in the game, try your best to maintain a simple view.

Step no. 3c: Bring a Game Strategy together.

We're trying to create a collecting game in this book. That's what I've been thinking about with my strategy so far.

- Theme: This game is about mermaids and will occur underwater.

- Control: A player monitors every movement of the character

- Objective: The goal is to move the player around and gather as many objects as possible!

Your strategy doesn't need to be very comprehensive. Everything I know so far about the game is that I'd like to move the character around and collect the objects. And that's enough to keep going.

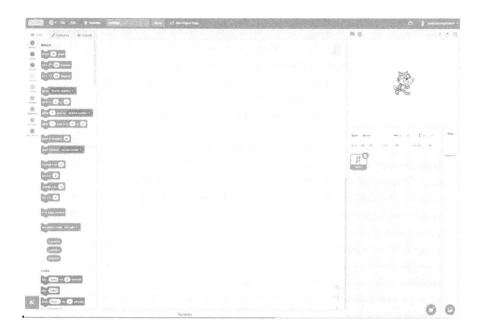

It is time to start writing the code. To develop a new Scratch project, navigate to the Scratch website and press "Create." It will lead you to a brand-new, unnamed Scratch project. The only thing you need to see is the cat in the center of your stage.

Step no.4: Create the lead character

Step no.4a: Build the sprite

Now we need to build a "Sprite" for the major character. Sprites portray characters and items in the Scratch projects.

These sprites are pictures, and they appear in the key area where the game begins in the top right, called the stage. Sprites will move around and run the code we send, which helps us build some pretty cool projects!

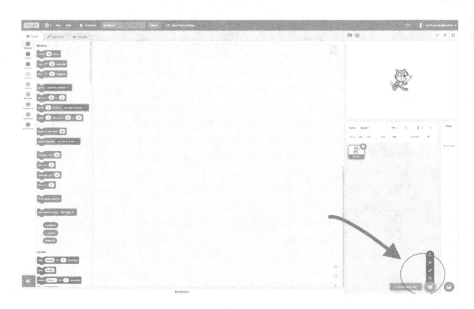

So far, the only sprite that the game includes has been the Scratch Pet, which is used in all projects by default. To build the new sprites for the main character, press the Choose a sprite" button in the lower right corner of your page.

Now from the menu, pick your key character. You may select from a collection of pre-made sprites or customize the game and paint fresh sprites yourself in either a costume tab or the paint editor. You can also upload your photo if you would like to!

We're going to use the mermaid as the first sprite for our game. It is one of the standard sprites inside this menu. You can notice it in the middle of the stage after making a sprite. The cat would be there as well— but if you don't want it in your game, you can erase it by clicking on the trash icon on its sprite.

Step no. 4b: To program the character.

Now that we have developed the new sprite, it's the moment to bring it to life! Since this sprite is supposed to be the game's central character, let's write the code to command it.

The code that you write will cause the sprite to move as the player presses the keys.

We expect the mermaid to be able to move around in our game. It shifts left/right/up/down as we click the left/right/up/bottom arrow buttons.

Code it: Please read the Scratch Sprite Motion for Newcomers guide to understand how to program the whole code.

Find out what the Scratch Motion Code brings us by pressing that Green Flag!

Step no. 5: Select a backdrop.

Before we go on to add a goal, first, let's improve our theme by inserting a backdrop. Although backgrounds are not required to complete the game, they add a little bit more character.

You can make a really nice game without them, but then the game will only occur on the white screen! Choosing a pleasant backdrop allows you to convey the game's idea and renders the game quite more interactive and enjoyable.

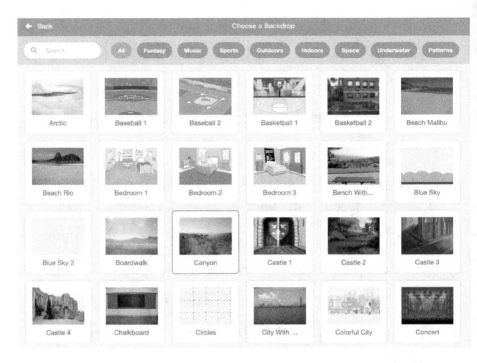

Press "Choose a Backdrop", the blue key in the right down corner. It will lead you to the background menu, in which you can pick whatever backdrop you like. You may even sketch your backgrounds or upload the photo from your device! To explore these and other options, press the respective buttons in a drop-down toolbar.

No matter what you choose, try to align the character and the background. For instance, if the central character is a warrior, you might use the castle as the background. It is going to express better the concept of the game to the user. Since our major character is the mermaid, our game will be played underwater.

Step no.6a: Pick the Sprite

Based on the strategy you created before, you must have a general understanding of the target. Games may have various goals.

Here are some of the goals examples :

- Collection Game: Things that you are expected to pick

- Dodging League: Opponents that you should stop

- Question Game: Queries to be addressed

You can pick your objective's sprite depending on the type of game you would like to pursue. For example, a question game may have a clever sphinx that addresses queries to the players. A dodge game may have a scary ghost chasing the player!

Collection game

A mermaid would need to gather pearls for our collection game. As she gathers one pearl, the next one will appear in a random place! Our score will boost by one point with each pearl we get throughout the game.

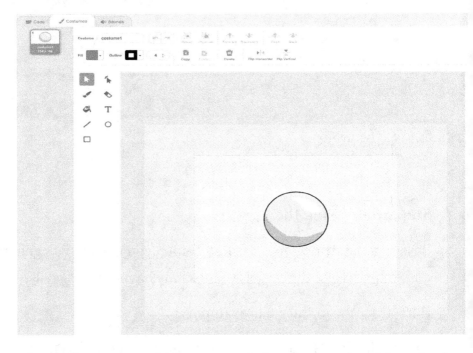

That's the sprite which we used for the pearl. Although the Scratch sprite library might not contain any pearl sprites, we created our own using the sprite editor.

Try and paint a fresh sprite for this move, or otherwise use another image.

Step no.6b: Write a code for the objective

When a mermaid touches the pearl, we expect another to show up in a random place on the desktop. It can be conveniently achieved by using the "go to the random position" block.

Here's a quick code view on how to make it happen:

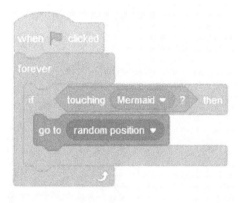

Let's go through what the code shows, step - by - step:

1. The game starts when you press on this green flag.

2. Just after the green flag is pressed, the pearl will verify whether the mermaid is touched.

3. If this is the case, it will move to a random place.

4. Steps two and three will be replicated indefinitely.

A forever block on the exterior is what is recognized as a loop. The loop keeps running every code you put within before the game ends.

It indicates that the pearl responds if the mermaid encounters the pearl; without that, the pearl can only verify this state at the beginning of the game.

Questions Game

Question games are different from collection & dodging games. Instead of letting the player switch and strike the sprite, we've got a sprite that asks questions about the gamer.

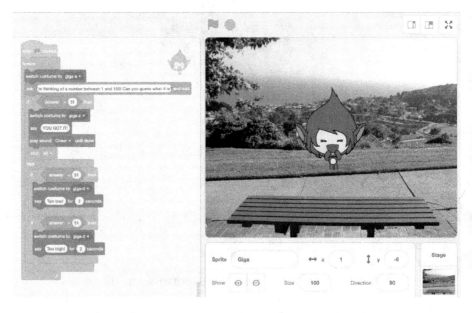

In this simple game, the code helps the sprite to pose questions about a game. They succeed because they get the right questions. The Light Blue question & wait blocks of Scratch will create a sprite that can do this.

Dodging Games

Dodging games involve the opponents you're supposed to defeat. The coding here is similar to the code we have already written above. To make sure that the player strikes the enemy, we have to provide the code.

The coding tends to succeed because if that bug strikes the cake in this simple game, you will not win!

If indeed the character encounters the enemy, you lose.

Step 7. Add some extra features!

Extensions to Scratch Game

Now that you have an easily controlled character and a functioning objective, the project satisfies all the game's essential criteria! If you've done this much, you may now claim that you've made a video game by yourself. Great job! Although your project is already considered a game, you can still develop it and make it more exciting to play.

This dynamic collection game has points, lives, and several sprites with different rules of interaction.

To make the game more complicated, such as this Ocean Cleanup game, consider incorporating components that fall into these categories:

- Extra targets

- Extra interactions

- Supplementary rules

- An extra challenge

Here are several examples of elements that come into the following categories:

Final Touches

Finally, there are a few non-essential changes that can make our game more enjoyable to play. These cosmetic modifications can be made to every project and are just going to make the game better!

Try to incorporate these add-ons on your own:

- When you collect an object, insert a sound effect, by simply adding in the soundtrack as you play the game

- Changes of costume

- Introduce more sprites to the game

The simplest change that you can make to any game is music. By using the Scratch sound blocks, we can introduce all sorts of sounds to the game.

Another improvement you might make to your game is a costume change. We can command the sprite to "switch costumes," which will introduce features like walking or moving in animations.

More Advanced Gaming

Discover other examples of more sophisticated games that you can create! Later on, we'll speak more about how to apply these complicated features to the games.

Use Physics: this collection game uses basic "physics" rather than stationary objects, cheesy puffs being continuously dropping from the sky!

Adding a timer and scoring system: the dodging game places the player in charge of the umbrella and in this example the goal is to use this umbrella to hold the baby chick (sprite) dry and maintain the "Missed" counter as small as possible!

Adding life and modern mechanics: this complex game blends several common mechanics. The player controls the character with the arrow buttons, and the aim is to search the cave and obtain the riches while responding to the questions correctly.

4.5 Step by step, the polygon robot in Scratch

Depending on variables, like range of values, radius, arc, pen color, pen size, this software can draw various designs.

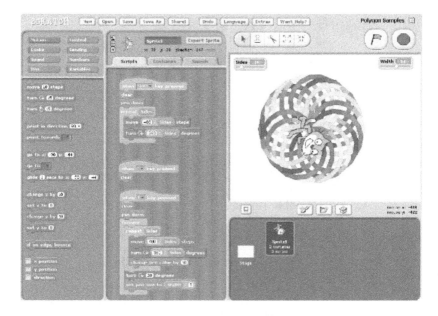

Open Scratch, then Simple script draw-a-square:

1. Select Button Scratch one time.

2. Holding the Cat. To draw a square, insert the scripts that follow.

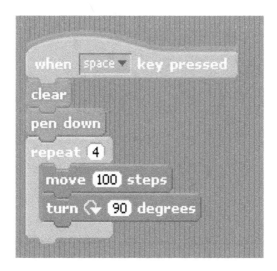

Shift Square Script to Creator Polygon:

3. Tap on the Tab for Variables.

4. Click "Create a variable."

5. And in Dialog Box, write "Sides" and press "Yes."

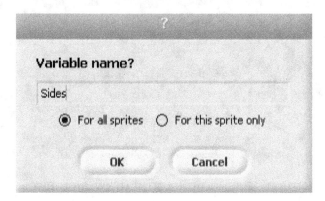

6. To build a Slider, twice-click the 'sides' box on the globe. Configure the Slider six.

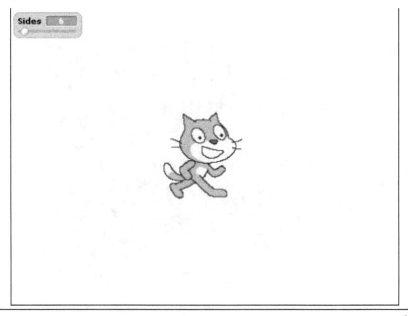

7. In a scripts window, move the data Sets. (Under "Figures," the green division is noticed)

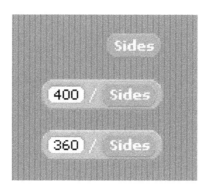

8. Throughout the square script, placed these blocks.

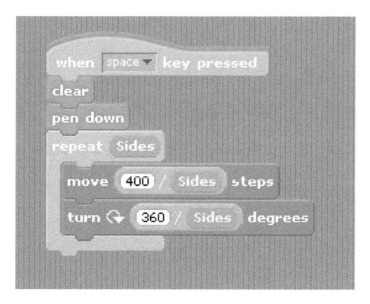

9. Click the bar for rooms. The Cat has a hexagon to draw. To produce numerous polygons, move the slider down & up.

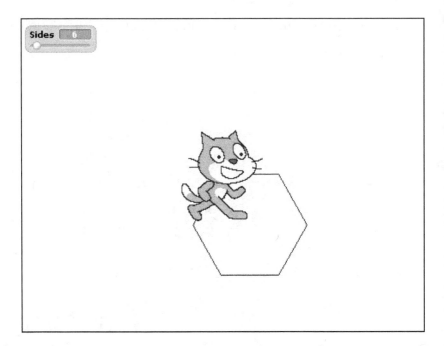

Render the script for the flower created:

10. Tap on Variables, and then make "Distance" a key.

11. Beneath the Square Script, render the following document

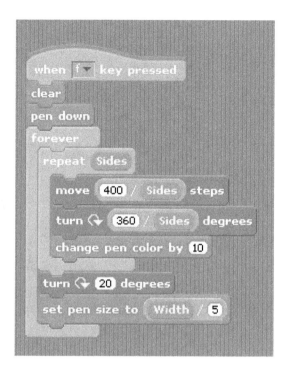

12. Press the "f" keys and create some interesting patterns for your pet. To halt the pet, press the Stop Sign.

Adding some more variables:

13. Move to a variables tab, and then apply the variables that attach.

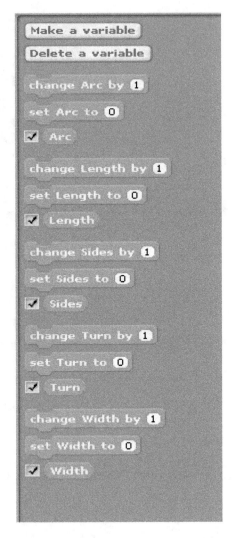

14. To appear like this, modify the flower script.

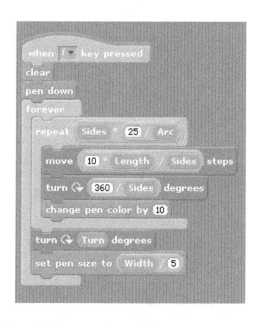

15. Dbl clicks all variables so that sliders are open. Creating any designs.

16. In your folder area, save your work as "last name polygon".

17. Currently, the left arrow is going to work! To have the Sprite look in the right direction, press the only flip left-right button.

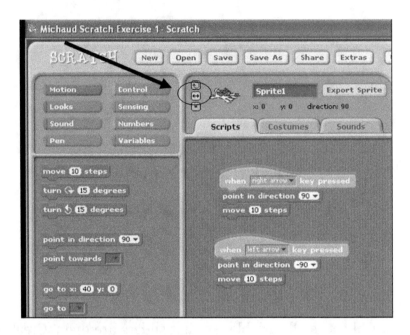

18. Drag & link the below tiles: Let your Sprite step down:

a. "As he pushed 'Space.'

b. "point to '90' route."

C. "10 steps pass."

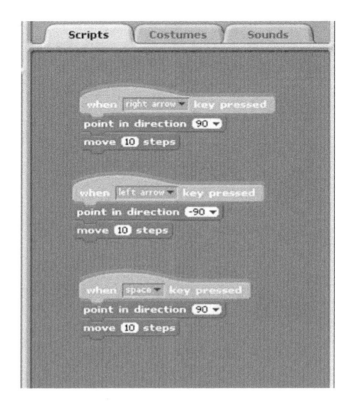

22. Set a downward direction:

A. Shift 'Room' to 'Arrow down'

B. Turn 'Ninty' to '180'

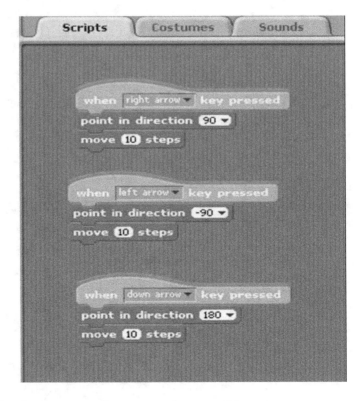

23. The down arrow is expected to work!

24. Push the link the following tiles: Let the Sprite go up:

a. "When pressing 'Room.'

b. "point to '90' route."

c. "10 stages pass."

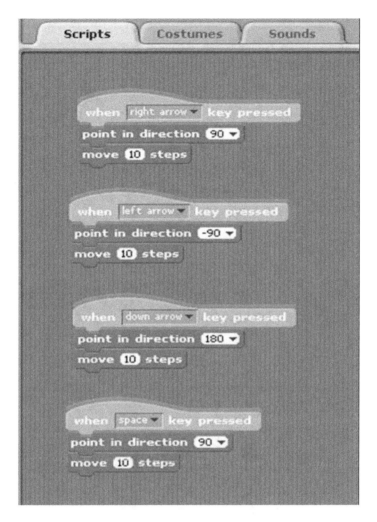

25. Setting the upward direction:

a. Shift between 'room' and 'up arrow.'

b. Modify '90' to '0'

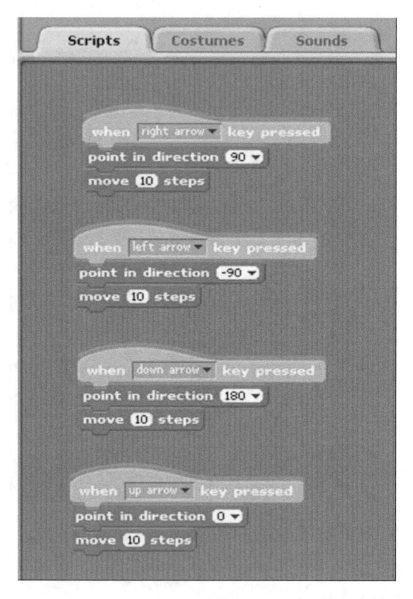

26. Now, it seems to be easy for the Sprite to travel across all four directions! By dragging your sprite across the computer, evaluate your program.

27. Change the name "Eater" as the Sprite.

28. Save your work!

4.6 Soccer game

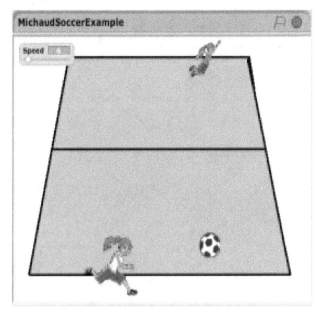

1. Change the script and outfits to let the character track right and left having the X position mouse.

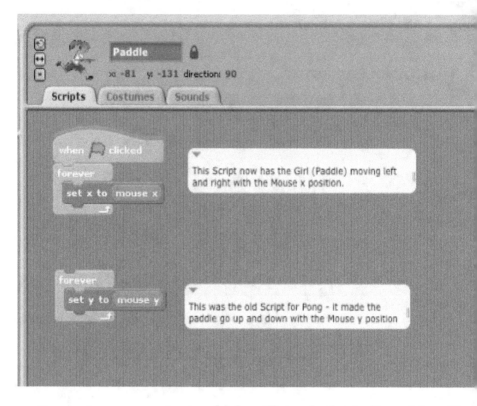

2 .Generate a competent, which will track the ball position X automatically.

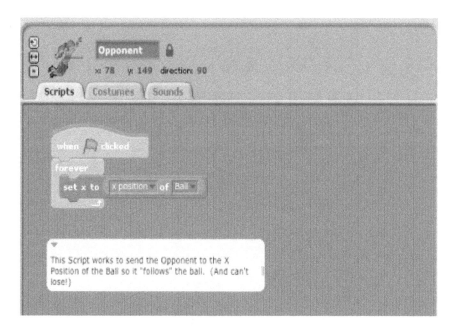

3. To change the ball for a smaller one when it travels to the edge of the frame, adjust the ball script. "Besides, introduce a or" declaration in the conditional on causing the ball to jump off the "Paddle" as well as the "Opponent." (Not required, but it gives for a fun "3D" look.)

Adjust size of ball to make it get smaller as it goes towards the top of the Screen. This simulates a "3D" depth of the soccer field.

4. Remember, I added speed as a variable that permits the developer to control the ball's pace, scratch

---

4.7 Dodge

Complete guidance is given below.

Step 1: A short recap on Scratch

. In Scratch, there are four essential items that you have to understand:

- Sprites

- Script

- Blocks

- Level or Stage

These Scratch extensions have special blocks from which you can monitor the evive in Scratch:

Arduino: These blocks regulate the fundamental input, output, and connectivity such as optical and analog input/output, PWM output or serial communication, etc.

With this Block, one can monitor the basic tasks of the device, such as a 5-way navigation key, Touch switches, Slide switches, Touch inputs & Real-time clock, potentiometer, motors, using this Block.

EvivetFT display: This Block could manage the TFT monitor of evive.

Eviveapp: You can connect with a smartphone app by this Block.

Evivetinkering: Such blocks are used to link separate sensors & actuators to each other.

There are 2modes in Scratch in which user can work:

Arduino Mode: The command blocks will be passed to Arduino C++ for Arduino IDe within Arduino mode, or the developer will change the code in the Arduino IDe then execute code to the robot. A Robot is working offline in that situation, but it cannot communicate with the level of Scratch.

Scratch mode: Within Scratch mode, the default when mBlock begins, mBlock can program the robot via USB serial port, a robot can connect with mBlock, or the robot can interact with the stage build more fun designs and animations.

We use step & sprite in the current project, so we have to work in the scratch form to use the Block that detects keyboard input.

Step 2: The animation of running

If you are not acquainted with constructing and integrating backdrops & sprites visit the game or any tutorials, such as:

• Sprite & Stage

• In Scratch, how can I create animations?

If the kid's sprite in the library is not accessible, try to download it and then the school scenery background.

You will quickly build a running script.

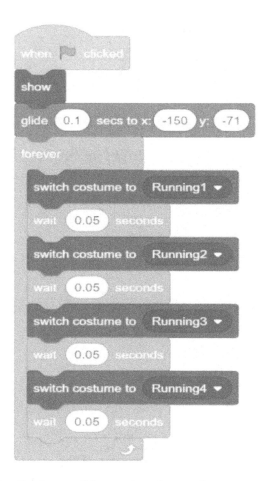

By moving the Sprite and lowering it to where you want it to be, its X and Y connections can be calculated. A glide block immediately reads such coordinates.

Be careful not to put too much of the Sprite on either the bottom or top half of the level. The greyest place on the road is an optimal location.

Step 3: Jumping

Now, let us compose scripts to support the boy hop and fall. In the center, the costumes reflect when the guy is in the air, where the ist and final present the start and the end of a leap. The second and fourth costumes reflect the corresponding occasions it is linked to take off & touchdown. At the same time, the third suit reflects the jump's maximum points.

Note that this is crucial. Since we are leaping, the sprite can stay in the air for a little more time than on the ground.

Another point worth mentioning is that your Y-coordinate can grow as you turn from one-> two and two-> three only with Y connect for the third costume providing the maximum Y-coordinate (max) as you change costumes.

Step 4: Sliding

The following pictures show the sliding processes. Again, each costume's period and height must be carefully controlled so that it might be possible to move under the aircraft. Note the added time that the sprite spends (in secs) in costumes three, four, and five when the kid appears like he's sliding.

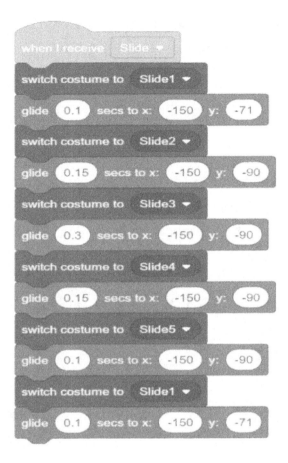

It is ok if, for now, you can't calculate the duration the sprite lasts in each costume. When you operate all the scripts, the requisite period can be changed, and you will get an approximation for how long it would take you to hop over the ball, slip under the aircraft.

Step 5: Synchronized running, leaping, and sliding

To clear hazards and move at all other moments, we can hop and fall. We need this for the three scripts to communicate with each other: "Rolling, Walking, and Slipping." We'll make adjustments to a running script to "see" when to trigger the leaping & sliding scripts. Then Leaping and Sliding scripts begin aside the block "When I get". We can verify if Evive 's tactile click 1, tactile click two is pressing, and then hop or slide accordingly.

The query is: how will this be done? Don't worry because Scratch has the needed blocks.

1. We will click the tactile switch to hop or fall while the character is in either of the moving costumes.

2. There's also the tact switch pressing Block within the Robot palette underneath the apparent expansion of inbuilt functions.

3. We realize we need to hop; now, we need to trigger the Jumping Script. Using the if section for this, but use the display and wait for the section to broadcast jump.

4.Drag & fall the hat block within the events palette. Adjust the message's name to "Check User Feedback" and snap just below the above script.

5. Can a message be submitted to verify user input? Yes, you predicted it correctly, as early as you turn costumes within the script for Running. You will observe that even after switching costumes, you are transmitting the post. It is achieved when playing to decrease the lag. You should try the other so that you could discover on your own. Also, build a 'Rate' variable to maintain track of your results. Scores ought to be 0.0. at the beginning of the game.

6. Try running this to see whether each time the sprite jumps. Similarly, for slipping, building bricks. The full User Feedback Search script is displayed.

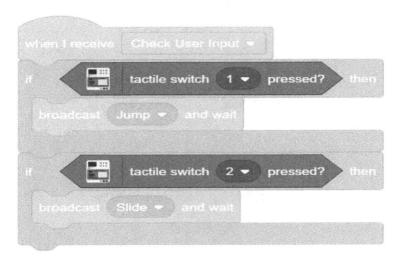

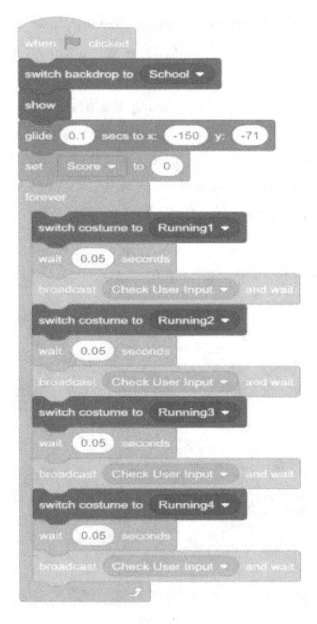

Please verify everything you have written so far. Check the scripts to see if the player (boy) is performing the acts needed.

Step 6: Spontaneously spawning the ball and aircraft

Now is the moment for the hurdles. We haven't installed our plane or our ball so far. Instead, we just determine at what moment they're going to appear on stage. We're going to pick an arbitrary interval of time over which the aircraft and ball look. See below for the script provided:

We must wait for 1 to 5 secs for a randomized time frame. Then, we desire to see some of the balls or the plane; we choose one of the two randomly.

The corresponding scripts underneath the ball & the aircraft sprite are triggered based on what is chosen. Now we're going to compose the scripts both for the ball & the aircraft.

Step 7: Plane script

Hold the Y-interlink constant and move the plane to the same location at other ends, beginning via the right side. Only at the end, remember that the aircraft has to disappear. Hence, at the end of the story, we hide it. We'll also show the plane after heading to the start point. Any time the plane crosses the boy safely, the score would raise by 1. An invariable palette, we execute this using the transformation block.

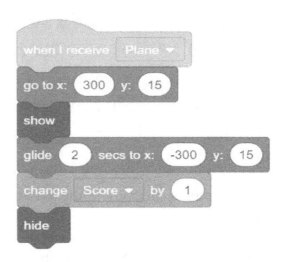

Step 8: Ball script

Next, a script is prepared for the ball. Begin your ball at (240,0). Do not get puzzled; at -120 (Y-connect) is the floor level (at which man's feet are).

Since the ball needs to bounce on its path until slowing down, the coding is a little complex. To maintain track of location and velocity (in the horizontal and vertical directions), we establish variables X, Y & speed.

1. To reach the boy, we require the ball, so we hold a constant velocity in the x-direction, tell thirty. We choose a negative signal since the velocity is to the left.

2. The following measures will be replicated until less than -ve240 is the X-coordinate, e.g., the leftmost side:

3. We say that at a pace of -ve30, the ball can travel 30 units per second to the left. Thus we shift the X-coordinate each time to -30.

4. At first, we desire the ball to drop down at the height and bounce up until it hits the ground. Developers do not, nevertheless, want it to increase to the same altitude, e.g., the (Y) speed of the ball can decrease until it bounces.

5. We must give it pace in -ve Y direction (downwards) for a ball that falls and adjust the Y coordinate accordingly.

6. However, if the ball hits the deck, we do not expect that to

happen, e.g., Y= of -120. We assign it an upward pace slower than the speed it dropped (by the 1.4 division).

7. Just to ensure that the (object) ball does not sink below -ve 120, as early as that occurs, we set its Y correlates to -120 again.

8. Whenever the ball crosses the boy safely, the score can raise by 1.

9. We also like the ball hidden at the last of the script and revealed at the script's beginning.

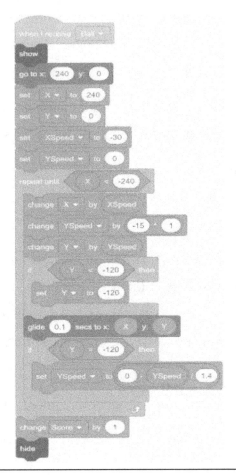

Step 9: Game finished

Now, we can see what occurs when the game is over, i.e., the boy has been hit by either the airplane or the ball. Before the game ends:

1. A message is shown by the boy stating he is hurt

2. On the school background, all action ceases.

3. The backdrop changes to GAME OVER

The script of the boy

We're going to verify whether the boy is hitting the plane or the ball. We're going to advertise GAME OVER in the texts after that. It will inform some other characters that their corresponding 'GAME OVER' scripts would be performed. We're just going to let the kid tell, 'Ouch! "I'm hurt" masks the backdrops of sprites and turns.

To prevent bugs, we use "stop other scripts in sprite". This one is available in the stop block of the lower down box.

The ball & the airplane

When the ball accepts GAME OVER, other scripts are interrupted, the ball is covered and sent to its starting point: (240, 0).

For the aircraft, too, the very same script is composed, just that its initial point is distinct from that ball.

Also, the characters, the ball and the plane should go to their original location when you begin the game and ought to be invisible. The template for the same thing is provided below.

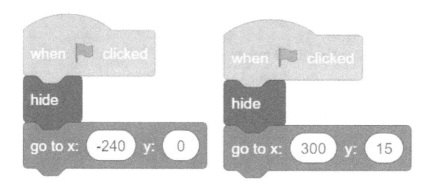

And there's a complete and available game to enjoy.

To change the game, for more simple or difficult, you can change the pace of the moving objects.

4.8 Music project

A Music Project is a program where its main role is , of course, music. It may include music files uploaded or Music created or captured with the Scratch software.

Music videos, Interactive instruments, and games featuring striking hitting or playing notes in series to form a song (called rhythm games) are famous music projects. Images or recordings of Scratchers or other musicians performing Music are also the other types of music activities. Music theory or tuning requires several substantially less common forms of the music project. Music projects are not called games with Music in the background.

4.9 Types

1. Interactive Instruments

There are 21 different timbres of the instrument that can be used in the Scratch software. The users can select by themselves which one they prefer.

Scratchers may also record themselves with the microphone of the Scratch program for more realistic sounds.

2. AMV

An AMV is an animation formed around the lyrics and melody of a song performed in the background, or "Animated Music Video". On Scratch, they are very prominent and sometimes enter the front page.

3. Recordings

In terms of style and genre, recordings vary: they can be instrumental or vocal, classical, or pop. Often, they are treated as covers.

4. Music from Games, Movies, or TV shows

Some projects reconstruct Music from sports, films, or television shows. This process can be carried out by using sound blocks or using audio or video. There is no need to confuse this form of music project with game projects that generally include playing Music in the background.

5. Reverse Music

Some programs, often created for entertainment or humor, play current songs in reverse. It is achieved by using the Sound Editor. There will be added "lyrics" in some reverse music programs to refer to "back-masking" which is another music technique.

6. Self-Composed Music

Some Scratchers create and launch their own Music on Scratch. In a computer program, Music may be produced and recorded.

7. Note Block Projects

Some users like to create Music by taking full advantage of their sound blocks in Scratch. Users can create scripts using music blocks that play-in series. Chords can be created by multiple scripts played together.

8. UTAU Songs

Most of the Scratch users have developed their UTAU characters and posted songs featuring them. UTAU is a free and popular singing app named after the Japanese word that means "To Sing."

4.10 Role-playing game

It is also abbreviated as RP or RPG in Scratch. You can play them in the Collaborations forum, studio, and project. These were played in the old Games Forums, which were only text-based before. The rules and format of this game in Scratch is not like actual RPGs, so this game should be called a storytelling game.

RPGs contain events where the user manipulates all the characters and let them communicate with others in a simulated world. Posts show short clips of a storyline, for example:

RPGer1: *"Mia went outside to check the area for intruders."*

RPGer2: *"Evie made a few mugs of hot chocolate. 'Mia, want some hot chocolate?"*

RPGer1: *"Yes please," Mia replied, taking one of the mugs and sitting down. She scanned the horizon for people as she took a sip of the drink.*

RPGs in Projects

If RPGs are made in projects, that project is developed and submitted by the Scratcher that owns it. Typically, the project provides details regarding the RPG as well as its characters. Other Scratchers comment on the uploaded RPG project, much like comments on a forum post. Projects' comments can be used by RPGs as sources of character details or other material.

RPGs in Studios

Many Scratchers favor studios over projects to create RGPs. As you can form several projects associated with the RPG in the studio rather than just one. Since the studio itself can never contain a project on it, the RPG information is put in the notes of the studio.

People can play RPG by putting comments in the studio notes similar to projects. See the following examples:

- Warriors of the Forest

- Anthros Unite

- Jigglers Role Playing Game

RPGs in the Text-Based Games Forums

Limited amount of comments can be made under the Projects in Scratch and studios, whereas the forum posts in Text-Based Games Forums do not have such limitations. But forum posts use formatting (BBCode) to simply quote the posts of others. Flag RPG was among the most famous RPGs in the TBG forum and became a topic with maximum posts on the Scratch website. But it was mysteriously deleted; that's why it does not have that title anymore.

RPGs were so popular on TBG forums that they had to divide it further into two forums on February 1, 2011, with only one whole forum dedicated to RPGs. Nevertheless, the TBG forums were shut down forever on March 1, 2013.

Basic Rules in RPGs

Some of the basic rules followed by most RPGs are as follows:

- There should not be any god-like powers and should not go beyond the rules of RPG.

- There must be no Super flawed characters

- There shall be no power playing — that means regulating the other characters.

- No flawless characters — meaning characters are flawless in every way. Such as "Gary Stus" or "Mary Sues"

RPG Accounts

RPG users can choose to build a different account with the username of the character they're playing. (For example, the BenFarmer account can be created by a player playing Ben Farmer.) Users can post projects created on these accounts to seem like they are developed by the character they play even while posting/commenting in their RPG. They would probably have an image as the profile picture of their character. These are mostly not used as primary accounts, although certain individuals are very interested in them. However, these accounts are frequently either removed or abandoned by the time that the RPG is finished.

Role-Playing Game Tutorial

RPGs typically have a single or several playable characters who are led on a journey through a world full of enemies. They are generally played from a top-down point of view.

How to make a top-down RPG will be shown in this tutorial.

Movement

One of the most fundamental scripts in an RPG is motion. With the arrow keys, this script will govern the player and end when the player reaches a black wall.

1) Basic Movement

The basic/fundamental method that can be used is shown here.

Good timing can allow someone to "clip" into the wall by using this detection method and walk around easily by clicking the arrow opposite to the direction they like to go. Also, a new way wherein the background shifts when the sprite hits the end and moves the sprite to the other end is the only way to get to places outside the view of the screen using this process.

Scrolling Movement

This is a more complex movement approach in which the player remains centered, meanwhile the background changes, giving the player an impression of moving. You can see it in some RPGs (e.g., Pokémon), they are quite popular but also can be more difficult to make.

Some sprites and parameters are required in order to make floating movements:

- Background sprite (one theme for each complete screen of background)

- Established the backdrop to the color that stops movement

- Character sprite

- ScrollX variable

- The private name for the background character: CloneID

4.11 Jigsaw puzzle game

A puzzle game is a style of game that is found on Scratch. This genre focuses on integrating game mechanics while pushing the

player to engage with them to achieve an objective in imaginative and mysterious ways. A jigsaw puzzle is a form of puzzle in which one integrates pieces to create an image. Jigsaws usually range from just four bits to hundreds of pieces.

Build the pieces first. Any painting editor can be used to create them.

Then, on each of the puzzle pieces, put these scripts:

Lastly, allow it to be pulled. Just click the blue color "I" close to the thumbnail of the sprite, then enable it to be dragged on the player.

Story Projects

Any project in which a story is being told is known as the Story Project.

These projects range from fun stories, where the scratchers create their own story, to animated talk shows, where animated creatures talk to each other. They are pretty uncommon as they belong to the category of animations.

Most of the story projects, particularly those which are non-interactive and fixed, are works of fiction, stories that use personalities and situations from a work of fiction but are produced by fans, not the scratcher or creator.

Interactive Stories

There are projects where a developer is provided with a selection of alternatives. The story will advance when they pick one. This gives the person the freedom to "create their favorite story." The "Choose Your Adventure" programs are also called active projects. These projects generally take rather more time than other story projects since it is important to create an interaction tree and program every potential outcome. These blocks are widely used to do that:

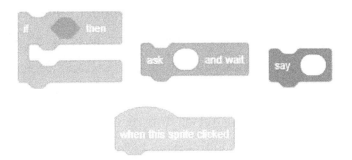

Often, an interactive story can allow users to comment on ideas for the next thing to happen. They are also being called 'projects of collaborative stories.'

Talk Shows

In these programs, using texts or programmed speech bubbles with the Says block, two or maybe more sprites speak to each other. These story projects are popular because they are simple to design for a new Scratcher.

In these works, a very popular block used is the block.

It can be used to let every character know when it's their time to 'talk'.

Books/Short Stories

These are projects in which the developer types his own story / short story for reading by other users. They might be long, or they might be super short. They may have sound effects or songs, but they really do not need them. The story is normally typed in the background(s) or sprite(s). You can see below a typical script used to switch pages with arrow keys:

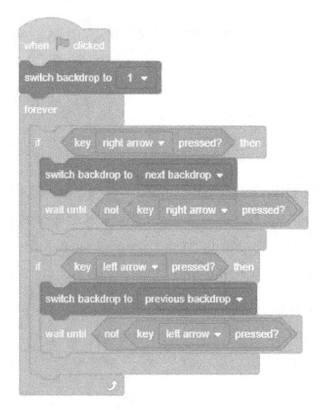

Making Story Animations

Creating a story animation is a type of work that involves a story to be animated and because of that it is needed to have some experience with the paint editor.

1) Obtaining an Idea or Storyline

Getting an idea is the first step in creating an animation of a story. When needed, they may be in chronological order. In the present or the past, or entirely fictional, you can choose.

Inspiration for drawing is usually the hardest part of the project. Many animators spend lots of time worrying about the "right" concept needed for an animation to be made. However, using

something simpler can be more satisfying for the beginner. It might take a long time to get the "right" concept, and it would be easier to pick one basic theme and just stick with it.

It can be a difficult challenge. Inspiration from many other sources is generally helpful in letting the imagination flow. Another potential way is to watch cartoons or read comics. A good way to start is to create a character rather than a story around the character. The characters don't have to be "perfect." They are even expected to be clumsy, make errors, or be the villain.

Chapter 5: Drawing tools for Scratch

5.1 Common options

All these are placed above the costumes/outfits. Both the bitmap and vector editors are familiar with all of the costumes.

Gradients

There are four choices on top of each three sliders. These allow an area to be blended among the two colors you have chosen. If one of these choices other than the solid color is clicked, two chosen colors will be shown. To edit them independently, click on each one of them. When you use any of the two options to cover an area, it is called the gradient.

Picking Colors

There is a color drop-down menu in the Scratch paint editor with three sliders that can be used to select colors: saturation, color, and brightness. It is located on the editor's center-left page.

Brightness

This option gives you a chance to choose how dark or light the color will be. When the right side is the chosen color, the left side remains black.

Color

Moving a color slider changes the color (from blue to red,

for example). As it shows the greatest differentiation between colors, this method is very commonly used.

Saturation

Saturation describes the intensity (purity) of the hue. It tells us how bright the color is. For example : 100 saturation will be of the chosen color, 50 saturation will be of a lighter color, whereas 0 saturation will be white.

Changing Pen Size

The pen size bar can be found in the center of the paint editor. The paintbrush icon represents it. Type in the size or change it by using the arrows on the side. The greater the number, the wider the line is going to be.

Choosing a Color

You can find an icon on the bottom right that enables you to select any color from the given costumes, it is sometimes known as an "eyedropper." When you move the mouse-pointer near the color it will magnify the area. Click to choose the prefered color.

Naming Costumes

Just click on that text bar located at the paint editor's top-left side to name a costume. The costume name is critical in coding. It is not a good option to name the costumes by using only numbers , it's better to use also other symbols or letters because it can create confusion and mess things up during the selection of your costume blocks.

Copy and Paste

There are two options on the right side of the outline: paste/copy. This copy option only copies the specified region and the paste places it anywhere the person wants. It is really useful when you want to make a copy of any object. The shortcuts used for copy is Ctrl+C, and for the Paste is Ctrl+V, you can use them here too. When a selected text or object is copy-pasted, the copy's location is different from the initial selection. So, to paste the content in its desired place, follow the below-given steps: (1) copy the selection, (2) change to another costume, (3) go back to the original costume, (4) paste that copy part before making any other modifications.

Redo and Undo

Two buttons named undo and redo located on the right side of the costume's title. These buttons enable you to do it as if the final operation never took place. It's impossible to use the redo button until the undo button is pressed. If no steps have been performed, neither option can be used. Ctrl+Z is the shortcut key for the undo and you can use it here too.

5.2 What are the vectors?

Vector painting is different from drawing with the normal paint application. Vector pictures appear flawless no matter how much they are zoomed in or out. There seems to be no pixel distortion here. Vectors produce a flawless and polished product of any dimension. You already know that in Scratch, the customizable characters of the game are called sprites. Scratch provides a sprite library that can be used, but you can still create your own using the built-in paint software or even the built-in vector application.

No drawing expertise is required to draw using vectors. Rather than sketching the object in one shot, you can split it into various shapes. Choose between squares, triangles, ovals, and rectangles. It may be beneficial to use images or a live model of an object that you are painting.

I will share with you all the key points of sketching a vector sprite in Scratch by demonstrating how you can draw the apple, but you can use this knowledge to any object you choose to draw.

Tools for drawing

You can find the Scratch's vector painting toolkit under the Fill & Outline icons. There's everything you need to draw the objects:

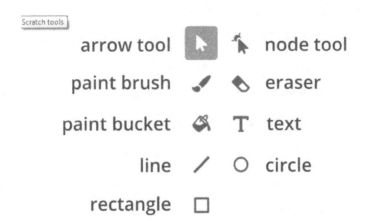

arrow tool   node tool

paint brush   eraser

paint bucket   T   text

line   O   circle

rectangle   □

Here's some of the terminology strongly associated with vector graphic's drawing:

Canvas: Where you can draw, the grey and white checkerboard appears translucent.

Node: The point in the path of the entity that defines the shape of the object.

Object: square, circle, or canvas line

Tool Arrow: Select, rotate, and resize items using the tool.

Tool Node: Insert, shift, and choose nodes by using the tool.

Get started

Open the website browser and move to Scratch.mit.edu to begin drawing. Open the program if you are operating Scratch

Desktop.

Choose to Create from the upper menu to launch the new project.

To open the Scratch Vector Drawing application, click that Blue Scratch Cat key, and then click the Paintbrush feature. It is going to build a clean sprite canvas.

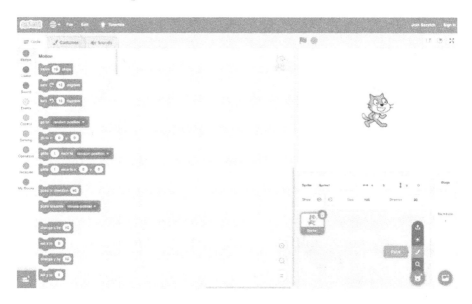

Draw the apple

Choose a Circle tool in an empty sprite canvas and make the circle by dragging the mouse. Holding the Shift button in the meantime will help you achieve a perfect shape circle. If you want to change the circle color, go to an Arrow tool, then click on the circle to pick it, and tap the drop-down list. It opens up to possible options for modifying the shade, contrast, and light intensity of your circle. If you choose a shape to be transparent, click a white box with a red diagonal line. If you'd like to add or delete a colored border around the object, go to the drop-down

Outline menu.

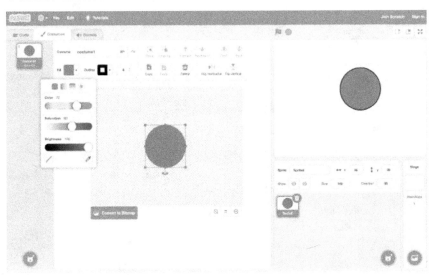

Choose a node tool. For selecting it, tap the middle of the object. You'll notice four nodes equally distributed along the edge of your circle.

The movement of any of the nodes would alter the shape of the circle. You may insert further nodes by tapping the edge of the circle. If you shift a node too far or add a node by mistake, you can of course reverse the last action by pressing the back arrow icon to the upper end of the page. You can also undo this by clicking Ctrl+Z.

Typically, the apples are smaller on the bottom than that on the top. Select and move the two side nodes. When clicked, the nodes appear blue.

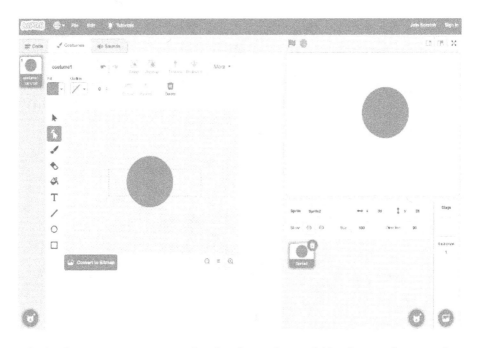

Click the Up Arrow on the keyboard to shift the nodes to the circle's top with your chosen nodes

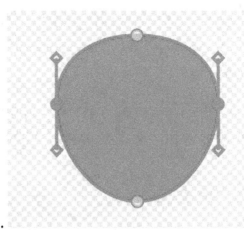

Insert two nodes to the bottom of the circle—one to the left of the initial lower node, the other one to the right side, as per the picture below. Now lift the initial bottom-center node a little bit up to generate an indent.

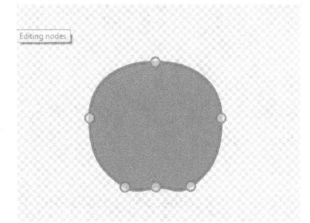

Now similarly, add the two nodes to the top of your circle. Lower the initial upper-center node marginally to generate an indent.

Continue to modify and insert nodes until you are satisfied with the shape of the apple.

Sketch the stem

Choose a rectangular tool. Try to make a rather long but thin rectangle on your canvas where you would like it to be.

You can use the same Node tool as before to form the rectangle to make it look like a stem. Adjust the fill to the color you want, I chose green as you can see below. If you want to move the stem just use the Arrow tool and if you wish to put it behind the apple click on the Backward key above the canvas.

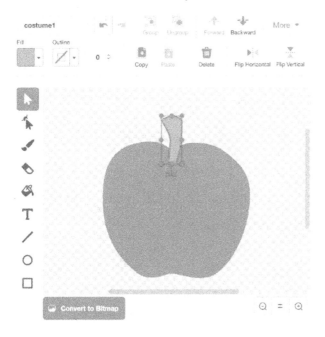

Highlights on the apple

To be able to apply this highlight form on the apple choose a Line tool. Draw a triangle on the apple, where you want the highlight to be ,by linking every other new line to the end of the former one. It is going to transform the lines into a full shape triangle. Select your new triangle using the Arrow tool and modify the color to a lighter one, such as white by using that Fill tool. You can use the Node Tool as before to make a nicer shape of the highlight as a sharp triangle is not very nice. Adjust it how you prefer. Curved button can help you achieve a better result.

Pro tip: To pick more than one node at the moment, press Shift when choosing each node. And exactly like that, you drew an apple.

If you wish to use the picture outside of Scratch, right-click on the costume thumbnail and choose Export. .It would download your drawing in an SVG format.

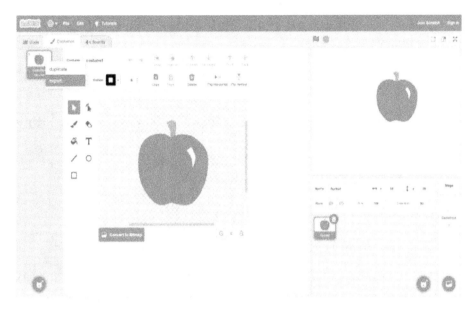

Come back to your code tab to use that picture in the Scratch project. The new sprite would show up in the right-hand corner with all of the sprites of its project. You can use that in the Scratch project, start sharing it with the other Scratch customers on the Scratch site.

5.3 Bitmap tools

Bitmap editor tools are identical to those of the vector editor but rather use a pixel grid on the region than spline formation. The bitmaps are usually pixelated because of that and also they don't have that many tools accessible.

Paint Brush

It's a tool for painting wherever you click with the mouse. You can easily change the color, scale, and the size of the pen.Go to the lower left side corner of the slider, and adjust it to the level that you like the most.

Line Tool

For creating straight lines, the line tool is used here. Holding the Shift key enables you to draw lines at ideal angles (such as -180 degrees, -45 degrees, or 90 degrees).

The Oval Tool (also called a circle)

The oval tool is called the "ellipse" or "circle." The tool is being used to create ovals of all shapes and sizes. By simply pressing the Shift key when designing, this tool gives you flawless circles.

The Rectangle Tool (Also called a square)

The rectangle tool for creating rectangles is simply the rectangle tool, generally known also as the "square tool". You can choose the color and the size of it as previously explained with the Oval Tool.

The Text Tool

Thanks to the nine available fonts you can write a text on a costume or in the background. Click wherever on your canvas when the tool is selected to let a cursor display. You can then insert the text into it. You must move the small cubes to the required size to adjust the text's size. You might also extend and condense your text with these keys, but it could only be accomplished after typing ends. You can only resize the text once.

The Paint Bucket

The paint bucket is used to fill the color into every closed area. It can be done by clicking on your canvas in the chosen place. The paint, which contains a similar color on it, tends to spread everywhere. The color might spill out of your form if the shapes have tiny holes in them. Before using this method, search for any gap and try to close it.

The Eraser

The eraser tool can be used to delete (or remove) a canvas area that has been selected. No color appears in the place of the removed colors, which means that the field becomes transparent. It should not create an outline, unlike the vector eraser. You can also change the size of the eraser.

The Selection Tool

This Select tool can be used to pick and move, extend and compress an area on the canvas. When the blue box appears around the selected area you can go on with all the changes. Additionally, you can rotate the object with a blue arrow in the section located on the lower side of the targeted area.

Chapter 6: Sharing the project over the internet

6.1 How to operate scratch software on the internet

Scratch's more about studying and sharing and the website (http:/)scratch.mit.edu) has been created to do so.

To make it easier for you to access and run the Scratch application software you should use the apps uploaded by representatives of a global Scratch group. You need to use a web browser that helps Java view and open Scratch programs on the webpage. To see whether Java is installed on the browser, check the Scratch homepage and tap on one of the several Scratch projects accessible. If an application opens, Java is installed and will surely work correctly. Otherwise, you should download Java, you can do so free of charge by accessing http:/www.java.com/en/download, pressing the Free Java Download key, and following the guidelines given.

6.2 Upload your Scratch app

The first move to share the Scratch app is to press Share! The button at the top of the Scratch IDE shows the window displayed in Figure Start by entering the account name and password, and then entering a title for the project. Second, write some notes that you believe other Scratch developers using the Scratch platform may like to know how to use your app. Scratch even promotes a labeling option that you can use to support other Scratch programmers. By default setting, Scratch allows you to pick any of the six predefined labels that cover the following components.

- Animation

- Music

- Story

- Art

- Game

- Simulation

You can also build as many as you want custom labels by providing keywords that you believe better represent your application. If you've done filling this data, press the OK icon, and the upload procedure will start.

Organize and View your application

Every Scratch app project you submit to the Scratch platform is saved on your website's home page.

You can use your app from here, post notes, add extra labels, and create galleries to organize better your apps. You may also remove any projects you posted and see feedback made by other Scratch groups' users.

6.4 Run your application

Once you upload it, you can see and organize the applications online by clicking on them. Once opened, you can deal with and execute your application the same way you also do when operating it on the local desktop. Surely, the green flag and the red Cease Everything icons are visible in the upper right corner of its online stage. Once started, you can also deal with Scratch apps using your keyboard and mouse.

6.5 Adding tags and comments

By uploading comments, you will exchange additional details regarding your Scratch submission. To do so, scroll down the screen to the "Add the Comment" section . You can type whatever text you like in this area and then press the Add key to post the comment. When uploaded, these comments, and also any comments posted by other representatives of the Scratch Group published on the application are visible.

6.6 Followers

Scratchers can follow each other by clicking on the "follow" button. It's a good way of appreciating somebody's work and also to be always updated with the new projects of this person.

Getting Friends

How to have more followers and friends? Offering a supportive and nice comment is a great way to make friends here. Instead of simply complementing that a project is "nice," "good," or "cool," it is recommended to include experienced and complete comments with input on the project.

Don't be scared to ask questions about how a developer has done something. Many people are glad to support other scratch developers.

And here is another list which would help you get a better view on you and your projects:

- Present yourself nicely

- Be kind and polite

- Grammar check

- Don't present yourself as Mr/Mrs " I know-everything".

- Leave nice and beneficial comments to others

- Ask questions

Note: Never accept to visit people in person, no matter how connected you feel to somebody on the Scratch website or any other website. Also, do not disclose any personal details such as an address or your identity. Always be careful!

6.7 Signature

A good signature can be a nice marketing tool. However, getting just text would make it very boring. A perfect way of keeping people involved is to have a photo commercial. It should involve an illustration that portrays the project in an entertaining way, and it's helpful to have a funny, catchy slogan. Don't forget to check the grammar!

6.8 Update the projects

If you decide to make changes to the project after accepting it you could do so by submitting it again, using the same title you have used to upload it for the very first time. If you want to keep the original copy of the project as it is on the Scratch webpage, you will have to allocate a different title to the updated version of the application before you post it.

6.9 Removal of projects

If you decide to delete any of the projects, you posted to the Scratch official site, you can do so by simply accessing the project list, choosing one or more of the projects and deleting it.

Conclusion

All of the chapters mentioned above have been written to help students understand how to create applications.

It's a nice opportunity to develop a wide range of skills. By working in pairs, communicating with other children in the family, watching the videos, and experimenting with coding and modifying apps, they will work on their comprehension skills.

Geometry and mathematics principles of angles & co-ordinates can also be expanded for older students. Turtle drawings and the technique of discovering forms and polygons through experimenting may improve the understanding of the topic in youngsters.

In reality, when Scratchers organize and do the team work, they study together many concepts during brainstorming. They practice creativity, communication skills and cooperation between the members of the team : all essential skills of the 21st century.